Follow the Blackbirds

FOLLOW THE BLACKBIRDS

GWEN NELL WESTERMAN

MICHIGAN STATE UNIVERSITY PRESS ▪ *East Lansing*

⊚ The paper used in this publication meets the minimum requirements
of ANSI/NISO Z39.48-1992 (R 1997) (Permanence of Paper).

 Michigan State University Press
East Lansing, Michigan 48823-5245

Printed and bound in the United States of America.

19 18 17 16 15 14 13   1 2 3 4 5 6 7 8 9 10

LIBRARY OF CONGRESS CATALOGING-IN-PUBLICATION DATA
Westerman, Gwen.
[Poems. Selections]
Follow the blackbirds / Gwen Nell Westerman.
pages cm
ISBN 978-1-61186-092-4 (pbk.)—ISBN 978-1-60917-384-5 (ebook)
I. Title.
PS3623.E84767F65 2013
811'.6—dc23
2012046616

Book design by Charlie Sharp, Sharp Des!gns, Lansing, MI
Cover design by Erin Kirk New
Cover art is "Return of Blackbird Woman" ©2012 Arthur Short Bull and is
used courtesy of the artist, all rights reserved.

g green press Michigan State University Press is a member of the Green Press
INITIATIVE Initiative and is committed to developing and encouraging
ecologically responsible publishing practices. For more information about
the Green Press Initiative and the use of recycled paper in book publishing,
please visit *www.greenpressinitiative.org*.

Visit Michigan State University Press on the World Wide Web at
www.msupress.org

Contents

All language is a longing for home.
JALALUDDIN RUMI

I.

Follow the Blackbirds

The last time I saw her,
confined to hospital bed
in compact tribal housing,
my mother's mother
lay evaporating before
my eyes.
I don't even feel alive,
she said.
She asked for water,
and between small sips
from a straw,
slowly smiled.
Grandma told us
to look for
blackbirds,
she said,
that they always
go to water.
You won't ever
be lost
or thirsty
if
you follow
the blackbirds.
Eyes closed,
I drink in her fluttering voice
trying to quench
the imminent drought,
as flashes of red and yellow
burn across a darkened view.
Don't forget me,
she said,

and don't forget
when you're thirsty,
follow the blackbirds.

A Trade

Following work,
I went west
from the Oklahoma hills.
Left my girl behind
with my mother,
and my two baby boys
in the ground.
It was 1939.
Being hungry was hard.
Being lonely was worse.
In Gallup,
a sign said
Waitress
Wanted.
The owner gave me
a crisp white uniform
with pearl buttons,
and new shoes.
Said pretty girls
bring in the customers.
I poured coffee.
Served pie.
Took short orders
and sidelong glances.
After closing,
I drank beer with the locals
until their suspicious
wives
dragged them home.
Married Mr. Wright
but found out soon
that he wasn't.

Moved on.
Flagstaff.
Barstow.
My girl went
to Marietta.
Chilocco.
I kept going.
The shipyards
in San Francisco
by 1943.
Welding on the
second shift.
Hard work,
long hours.
Good money.
At least the war
had some benefits.
Married Mr. Right.
A good-looking sailor
ten years my junior.
After the war,
he took work
with the railroad
and took me home.
Wichita.
Bought everything new
for our new life
together.
Furniture, dishes,
a house.
Work made it
home

but it didn't
seem like
work
at all.

School Days

A small cracked black and white picture.
School name and year
printed across the bottom.
Marietta 1940
She is barely six.

Mouth pressed in a line,
no trace of a smile
anywhere on her face,
her eyes black and full
of sadness.

Head tilted slightly,
straight black hair
cut chin length and held
away from her face
by a ribbon tied in a bow.

    Does it match her dress?
    No color in that world.
    No one left to ask.

The photographer tells her to smile, again.

    Does she already see
    the disappointments
    that lay before her?

The shutter clicks. Flash. Next.

A screen door slams. Mama? Daddy?

The matron tells her to stop crying, again.

Creaky hinges on a front gate draw her
to a window where she waits.
Mouth pressed in a line,
her eyes black and full
of sadness.

Innocent Captives

Captured blackbirds call their unsuspecting relatives
to a feast placed away from fields of ripening sunflowers.
On top of cages, brown rice glitters in toxic trays,
a tempting easy meal.

Poisoned.

Ancient memory guides them each spring and fall
along river valleys and wetlands where rich
cattail marshes were drained and fertilized for increased yield
and prized cash crops and condos grew.

In August, heavy black heads of sunflowers give up
their oil-laden seeds.
Beaks, sharp and black, split shells, black hulls fall
to the black ground.

Pale kernels swallowed in faith to nourish the migration

not all will survive to make the journey.

Husks drop and rice scatters, as darkness falls

blackbirds roost
in a flash of black and red
and they fall
silent
among the blooms.

Mourning Song
for Bud

Marked by a dotted green line on a tired map,
the scenic byway shimmers through the glimmering
heart of gold soybeans and cottonwoods in September.
Driving becomes mindless.
    Friend, pause and look this way.

Pushing up against guard rails and old cedar fence rows,
sunflowers stand in tribute along the blacktop,
inconsolable mourners along an endless memorial route.
Tires hum in harmony.
    Friend, pause and look this way.

A coyote slips up onto the crest of the road
and stops time on the center line when he looks over,
knowingly, then passes safely to the other side.
Our destination is the same.
    Friend, pause and look this way.
    The one for whom coyote sings is coming.

Dying of Thirst

leaves lose their weakened grip
and slip
yellow to the ground.

Linear Process

Our elders say
      the universe is a
         circle.
               Everything
         returns to its
beginnings.
But where do we go
      from here?
         Where are
               our beginnings?

               Our parents were stripped
               of their parents
               names tongues   prayers,
               lined up for their meals
               clothes   classes tests.
               When it was our turn
               to come into this world,
               they did not know
               what family meant
               anymore.
               They did not
               know.
               Yet even
             from here,
           we can
            see that the
           straightest line
         on a map
       is a
     circle.

Saving Scraps

I.

Side by side on a nubby brown couch,
they sat,
blue flickering light of a television
reflecting on their faces,
their eyes focused on their laps.
The old woman pulled a long scrap
of red cloth from a multi-colored
pile on the coffee table
and held it to the lamp.
Content with her choice,
she skillfully pinned
a brown paper pattern onto
the flowery red fabric.
She flexed her right hand.
It took only a few seconds to cut the piece.
The girl fumbled with a small
cardboard square, shifting and moving
and placing it just so
on the blue and white gingham
then poked her finger on the pin.
Without even looking at her,
the woman said,
Your mother couldn't ever
do nothin' right
either.

II.

This time of evening
was our favorite.
All day on my feet
and finally I can sit

for awhile.
Ten years now
that TV keeps me company.
I been saving scraps
and have enough now
to piece another quilt.
Flower garden this time.
These little colored pieces
fill my evenings.
Ten years ago
I made a quilt.
Khaki and denim and wool.
His work pants.
I held each pair
a long time
before I could rip the seams.
Cut big pieces
like his hands.
Smoothed each block
carefully
remembering his warmth,
his strong legs.
Stitched the pieces together
that winter
then tied that quilt with
red embroidery thread.
Each knot tied twice
to hold tight
what was left
behind.
Ten years now
since he held his only

grandchild on this couch.
His smile so wide
I laughed out loud.
Recovered
the chair and the couch.
But here she is,
a constant reminder
that he
is gone.
I sit here alone,
with bits of material and thread,
making something
out of nothing.

III.
The first letter I ever wrote:
        Dear grandma,
        I want to come live at your house.
        They treat me like
        I don't belong here.
        I put my clothes in my
        orange suitcase. Please
        come soon.
I was in first grade.
She came all right. She waved that letter
in my mother's face. I don't remember
what she said, just her figure framed
by the front door and sunlight.
Now I spend most weekends at her house.
She picks me up on Fridays after work
and we go to the grocery store
for potatoes, beans, and apple pie.

Mostly it's the same every time.
We watch TV and eat a slice of bread
dipped in milk before we go to bed.
On Sundays we go to church.
At night, when she thinks I'm asleep,
I watch the red ember of her cigarette
glow and dim in the dark.
She never smokes in daylight.
This time, she tried, again, to show me
how to cut quilt blocks, but the scratchy
brown couch makes me itch.
I poke my finger and it bleeds.
So many little pieces.
So many mistakes.

Dead End

Alone at the end of a dusty road,
withered cornstalks linger
like uninvited mourners
shrouded in gray and blue,
voyeurs now, abandoned
for more fertile pursuits,
weakened roots exposed,
they whisper of mistakes
and lack of rain and know
I can go no farther.

Early Freeze

I watch the moon creep
up beyond the trees.

Through the yellow glitter
of cottonwood leaves,
it slips into the darkened
palm of the sky.

As the horizon bleeds into dusk,
I run my hand
across the nap of the land
and feel frozen cornstalks
bristle across my palm.

Trying to piece together
what is left,
fingers numbed by a bitter cold
and unprepared for the sting,
I let the wind take my breath.

Henana Epe Kte

Look here, he said,
pointing to the ground,
a buck's toes
are farther apart
than a doe's,
that's how you know
the difference.
Remember that.

I remember.

Listen here, he said,
the easiest way through
the woods is on a path
that has already been
traveled by those who
went there before.
Remember that.

I remember.

Quantum Theory

Cut by a paper razor, I watch blood fill

    a perfectly straight wound on my finger,

Denying the swirl of generations before me and

    the possibility of those held in my dreams.

Illusory, the narrow and unyielding course fills

    in red, then overflows into a galaxy where

Blood carries stories of our origins from

    beyond the stars.

Genetic Code

On the edge of a dream,
the songs came.
Condensed from the fog,
like dewdrops on cattails,
they formed perfectly clear.
Whispering through leaves,
heavy voices rise up,
drift beyond night
toward the silent dawn,
and sing.

> *Hekta ehaŋna ded uŋṭipi.*
> *Heuŋ he ohiŋni uŋkiksuyapi kte.*
> *Aŋpetu dena ded uŋṭipi.*
> *Heca ohiŋni uŋdowaŋpi kte.*

Always on still morning air,
they come,
connected by
memories and
song.

22

Feed Them

They'll come back
to your dreams
and you can
help them.

That's why
they came to you
because they think
you can
help them.

There must be
a lot of good
in you.

II.

This Is My Explaining Ceremony

My strongest memories are of water. A rough rock ledge that reached out for the horizon beyond the lake, holding a perfect place to play in its palm. Cradled by the beat of waves washing ashore, I watched slick, black-green moss sway in clear swells, and was not afraid at four. Sounds of water comfort me.

At ten, I splashed through 14-Mile Creek with my cousins, turning over smooth stones and sharp rocks with flattened, shining forks tied to long willow sticks. We speared unsuspecting blue and gold crawdad treats hiding in the deep swift stream. Our grandmas gathered glistening green watercress for a summer feast, but a child with fast-food tastes, I refused to eat. Sounds of water connect me.

Near the old home place, my grandma said, the spring at Greasy Mountain never runs dry and the edge of 100 Highway always crumbles with each late winter thaw. I followed the black asphalt road as it snakes toward the turnout for the spring, and took my children there to drink the water, clear and cold. Sounds of water call me.

A grandma's words that can fill a rain barrel or wash away fences and fields like a flood. Sounds that bring life ticking on a tin roof, that sting bare legs and hearts. Sounds of water flowing. Sounds of water falling. Sounds of water filling.

Red Earth Gathering

A fine layer of red dust
settles on Cherokees, Dakotas,
Winnebagos, Hummers,
old Galaxy 500s, casting
chrome and rust and gold
and black and blue and green
and white
in the same
sanguine hue.

Indian Territory reclaims
the downtown parking lot
as it fills with sovereign
tribal license plates:
Cherokee, Osage, Otoe,
Muscogee Creek, Pawnee,
Wyandotte, Kiowa, Quapaw,
Apache, Cheyenne Arapaho,
Seminole, Ponca, Caddo.

Inside drums and voices pulse
dust from the rafters
of the Myriad Arena where
tiny tots strut and mother-daughter
teams float side by side
in streaming colors and
streaming video
as the MC calls for one more
intertribal to honor

the land, the nations, the people
who are the heart of
Red Earth.

Journey

I.
Learn the alphabet
a b c ç c' d e, no f
and then you can
say anything.

II.
Learn basic greetings
Toked yauŋ he?
and then you can
talk to anyone.

III.
Learn to tell time
Hekta oko
and then you can
tell stories.

IV.
Learn to share
Uŋspemakiya
and then you can
speak your heart.

V.
Aŋpetu kiŋ de
ake waŋçiyake
k'a
çaŋte mawaśte.

Flint Hills Release

for CFS

The Flint Hills at dawn blush
with pale pink light and memories.
Iron, Hatchett, Postoak,
Whitehorn, Coffey, you.

Golden black hair waves
over summer sweetgrass eyes—
a mixed-blood beauty in a dry land
of cast iron skillets and hearts.

Lightning strikes and a windswept fire
blazes through the tallgrass prairie
where words cut like a hatchet through kindling
gathered quickly before a summer storm.

In a barbed wire and post oak ring,
a love wrestles to break free,
but all that remains of the destructive match
are tangled sun-bleached white horns of elk.

A two-step that never ends
though the singing and drums disappear,
lost in the last wisps of smoke and coffee
around a Sunday campfire.

First Flight

From a towering
cottonwood tree, a young hawk
pleads for his next meal.

In a clear blue sky,
a soaring pair of red-tails
circles leisurely.

Their plaintive calls
echo, rise, and penetrate through
the river valley.

Mates for life, they beckon
from above the ridge line
for their only chick

whose unsure wings strike
the air and pull it beyond
the green canopy.

Prayers are lifted up,
gratitude carried high on
broad yet fragile wings.

Where the Buffalo Roam

The marks left by something that has passed
imprint the memory and the land.
Filled with life,
the ancient trails vein
through the tallgrass prairie
from valley to valley, age to age.

Buffalo drift unaware of the prime meridian
marked with barbed wire and fence posts.
Then given some latitude,
pulled by the tide,
they return to the
bluestem grass and coneflowers.

Near the Red River Valley, a small herd
escapes from a Minnesota ranch.
Buzzed by ATVs, indifferent to bribes of beets,
they turn in a defensive circle, protect the calves,
and stand their ground. Headlines read,
"Buffalo Refuse to Go Home."

Their migration route parts central Iowa
where corn flows in the Missouri River Valley.
At research stations, prairie is restored,
herds are managed. Along I-35,
buffalo calves peer out of pens and
sniff the captured wind.

Home on the range, shadowy bison
ride on license plates and
race across Kansas highways and history.
Slipping silently from state game preserves,

almost unobserved on ancient ocean swells,
the herd is carried far and away.

In the Okla humma sunset, ripening winter wheat
glows golden red against a darkened sky.
Acres for Sale, Prime Development, Master Plan—
behind a lighted billboard,
a buffalo bull stands
alone on a ridge.

Unaware that Interstates 29 and 35
follow paths from beyond time,
hypnotized by lines, lost without maps
drivers rush over fossils
still resting in chalk beds, past blurred hills
and fleeting memories.

From the edge of extinction, the buffalo know by heart
the tracks laid down by the millions
who passed in a dream, on an ocean, on a highway
and they watch over those held back by fences
just waiting, waiting,
waiting.

No Contest

On a dusty Sunday afternoon,
from my chair behind the drum,
I watch for a treasured smile
among the grass dancers.

Singers warm up a contest song,
and as the push-up sounds,
in a brilliant multicolored blaze,
they dance across the sun.

Swirling white and green and yellow,
like wind through summer prairies,
He dips and whirls along a path
set down to old-time rhythms.

Deliberate steps in measured time,
he moves among the men,
while judges watch with seasoned eyes
and score them on their style.

The last down beat will bring their
movements to an end, stopping
ribbons, roaches, beaded cuffs,
while heartbeats race ahead.

And on a dusty Sunday afternoon,
the contest ends the same.
Sweetheart, let me take you home
in my one-eyed Ford, again.

Linear Perspective

Once, out of the blue,
Lise asked,
"Are you a Robertson?
You look like a Robertson."
She was from Wahpeton,
she had seen a lot of them.
I told her,
"No, but we are related,"
and she laughed,
"Aren't we all?"

Poring over scattered pictures,
I tried
to find myself
among old albums, boxes, and books,
in the faces of our fragmented family,
through more than a century,
their eyes, their stance.
No one similar looks back,
except the faces of
my children.

Then, out of the blue,
my uncle said,
"I see our mother in you,
in your smile, and I hear it
in your laugh."
He nods his head in the backseat
as I drive too fast on I-5.
"No doubt about it."
I look in the rearview mirror,
and I smile.

Monet on the Northern Plains

*"It's on the strength of observation and reflection
that one finds a way."*
—Claude Monet

Late afternoon sun
changes quickly
on rolling hills and haystacks
much like it looks in
La Prairie à Giverny.
Geese glide over pale
wheat stubble rows
that end in waves of
cattail marshes.
Two horses nuzzle
in radiance across
a twisted barbed-wire fence
that tries to separate fields
of deep purple clover
and yellow mustard.
Hay bale herds graze
in roadside ditches,
along fence lines,
and in the
tawny shadows
of wind breaks.
Golden-tipped aspens
quiver in the breeze
as the last long shafts
of sunlight shift
from amber to
bronze.
Dusk deepens
the colors

and veils the view,
yet fleeting
glimpses
in constantly changing light
make
Wheatstacks and
grain fields
immortal.

Road Song

I left you there
and took only what
I could carry
a green tea kettle
filled with ivy
an Alvarez guitar
your gaze
and just over
that first rise
the prairie opens wide
meadowlarks whistle
on a fence wire
and I can breathe
again

Delisted

"Today I am proud to announce that the eagle has returned."
—Dirk Kempthorne, Secretary of the Interior, 28 June 2007

Forty years ago,
America's symbol was officially
protected under the Endangered
Species Preservation Act.
Ake wambdi kiŋ hdi.

Forty years later,
the bald eagle has recovered
from loss of habitat, deliberate
killing, and DDT poisoning.
Ake wambdi kiŋ hdi.

Forty-five years since
Silent Spring cried out for
an environment that could
not cry out for itself,
Wambdi kiŋ uŋkicidowaŋpi.

For longer than time,
the eagle has been sacred
and in our songs we have
asked it to protect us.
Wambdi kiŋ hdi.

Root Words

Prairie
grasses
have
roots
twice
as long
as their
height,
deep
footings
that steady
them against
unremitting winds
that sweep across
the plains. Their roots
reach beneath the parched
earth stricken by   heat and cold
and nourish   them on
the remnants   of a vast
inland sea   that
teemed with   copious sounds
of life long ago.
Our   language
is like those   prairie grasses
surviving   the fires
of missionaries   and their gods,
floods of   English words,
drought,   growing
in unexpected   places
as if it   had never
been   gone.

Daḳota wicoie
k'a iapi
teuŋḣiŋdapi.
Maka kiŋ etaŋhaŋ
uŋhipi. Ikçe
wicaṡta teuŋḣikapi.

At Spirit Lake

Where a million
white butterflies
flicker in
purple vetch,
stray sunflowers
edge asphalt and
cornfields,
the road dips,
curves south
and wheat meets
the horizon in
an embrace of
ripeness.
Against a
deepening sky,
stands of
weeping willow
hold throngs of
red-winged blackbirds
whose cries
pierce the
summer sky
and make
headless windmills
long to
sing.

42

Ḣe Keya Woabdakedaŋ

A cricket chorus

calls the moon to devotion where

flaxen blue sky blushes lavender.

Dragonflies rush to usher in the dusk.

Sunflower congregations bow their haloed heads

as a celebrant sun blesses

lush fields of wheat with radiance.

Grains fall upon the ground

and life springs up as a song,

I give you peace.

My peace I leave you.

Ḣe keya woabdakedaŋ.

III.

Venetian

Amid the crush and glare
of a Vegas escape
where sacred and profane blur,
a gallery offers refuge behind
a massive Italianate door.
In the last room,
a long marble bench
reflects the color field
of Rothko's *Untitled*
(Violet, Black, Orange, Yellow on White and Red)
when in a flash
as luminous
as vivid rectangles that
hover on canvas,
an image of home
shifts and shimmers,
like heat above asphalt.
Constituted and
reconstituted backgrounds
where we make and
remake
our selves
ourselves.

Skin Essentials

I.

They say
beauty is only skin deep,
but the aisles at Walgreens
overflow with promises of
astonishing immediate results!
Shelves, endcaps, bins spill
over with essences of everything—
essential fragrances, essential products,
essential needs.
Revolutionary, the box says, includes
essential oils
to make you think it's
the real thing.

Available for a limited time only
at a special introductory price.
And there amid the glamour and
the hype it beckons and gleams:
Skin Essentials—FREE after rebate!
Just send in the original receipt and
proof of purchase.
No cost.
No risk.
No sacrifice.

II.

Essence is a noun.
The intrinsic or indispensable
properties that identify
who we are—
eagerly grabbed by those who want
to capture the aura,

the basics of Indianness,
without the cost.
They mask their own deficiencies
with a light application of
shawl fringe and beadwork,
assumed names and
assumed authority.
Wash. Rinse. Repeat.
Repeat.
Repeat until
the fragrance covers the lack
of substance.
Prayers.
Relatives.
Ceremonies.
Connections to what is real.
There is an essence to who we are.
And a coupon from Walgreens
cannot be redeemed here.

Why He Teaches the Language

Sitting back in his chair,
eyes closed,
he listens
as a student struggles.
"Tok, toked,
toked yauŋ
he?"

Expecting correction,
hands clenched,
students wait
while he walks
through the past.
And he remembers
the pain.

Standing at attention,
head lowered,
ruler struck
a sharp blow
through his hands.
So he swallowed
his tongue.

Recalling the struggle,
heart lifted,
he smiles
and language breathes
through their efforts.
He treasures their words.
Wašte do.

Daḳota Odowaŋ

At the end of the Dakota-U.S. war in September 1862, nearly 2,000 Dakota people surrendered to the U.S. Army, believing that they would be treated humanely as prisoners of war. That November, 1,700 women, children, and old ones were forced to march 150 miles to a prison camp at Fort Snelling, an unknown number dying along the way and lost to their families, who were not allowed to bury them.

My flat English tongue
betrays my heart
and the songs of those
who came before
and who want to know
Daniḳota he?   *Are you Dakota?*

Early morning fog
rises from the Minnesota River
where women and children marched
November gnawing their hands.
Daniḳota he   *Are you Dakota?*
eya dowaŋpi.   *they sing.*

My hard English ear
struggles but my heart
hears their songs.
Odowaŋ kiŋ hena sdodyaye he   *Do you know those songs?*
Daniḳota he   *Are you Dakota?*
eya dowaŋpi.   *they sing.*

One hundred and fifty miles
they struggled to save their songs.
Nauŋyaḣuŋpi kiŋhan   *You will know them*
hena sdodyaye kte.   *when you hear us.*
Daniḳota ye   *You are Dakota!*
eya dowaŋpi.   *they sing.*

My healed Dakota heart
damaḳota ye dowaŋ.
Waŋna nawiçawaḣuŋ.
Uŋhdohdipi
eya dowaŋpi k'a
makicidowaŋpi.

sings, I am Dakota!
I hear them now.
We are returning home,
they sing, and
they sing for me.

Morning Song

As faint lavender light fills the river valley,
he leans forward and fully spreads his wings.
His bright red shoulders exposed with a flash,
blackbird summons spring.
Waŋ! De miye.

Full voice at dawn trills to claim the coming day
as the first rays of sun kindle his defending song.
Sheltered from the wind in a thick stand of cattails,
he has survived the night.
Waŋ! De miye.

His morning challenge echoed from among the reeds,
blackbird quickly changes his pitch in response,
and from upland past the edge of the marsh,
she answers his song.
Waŋ! De uŋkiye.
Waŋna mitakuye hdipi.

Winuna

First born girl.
First
born.
My girl.
Winuna.
Not
her name
but her place
in
my heart.

Wicaŋħpi Heciya Taŋhaŋ Uŋhipi
(*We Come from the Stars*)

Stellar nucleosynthesis.
That explains
where everything

in our universe

came from according to astrophysicists who
only recently discovered the cosmological constant causing
the expansion

of our universe.

Our creation story tells us we came from the stars to this place Bdote
where the Minnesota and Mississippi rivers converge,
our journey along the Wanaġi Caŋku,

in our universe,

that stargazers later called the Milky Way now disappearing
in the excessive glow of a million million urban uplights.
The original inhabitants of this place,

of our universe,

we are Wicaŋħpi Oyate, *Star* People
and will remain here as long as
we can see ourselves

in the stars.

The Lesson

for Arthur

Peaceful women linger above
in black-framed windows
and watch over his work.

Star women, wind women,
fleeting glances of delicate shades
gently gathered by a strong son.

Women reaching through the stars,
passing down spools of thread
to teach his hands to speak.

Through whispered colors,
he weaves their patterns
in swallows, wind, and snow,

and with faces hidden, they smile.

Tidal Force

The pale moon
drifts
on a breeze
while clouds
shift shape,
then dissipate
like good
intentions.

Tiny white
butterflies
dance and
hypnotize
the sun,
and celestial
mechanics
move oceans.

The strain
on earthly
bodies is
almost
imperceptible
as locusts
drone
their song

and we are pulled like the tide
toward home.

Owotaŋna Sececa

Hekta ehaŋna
    ḳaŋpi hena
        taku owas
            ecipaś
      hdi ce e
  eyapi.
Tka tokiya taŋhaŋ
    uŋhipi he.
        Toked kiya
           uŋyapi kta he.

          Ina ate kuŋśi uŋkaŋna
          wicayutakupida śni.
          Ikce wicaśtapi śni waŋna
          caże wicoie wocekiya
          kcihdaya nażiŋpi
          wotapi kte heyake toktokca
          wicapażo wicayuhapi.
          Hetaŋhaŋ uŋkicaġapi
          tka tiwahe taku sdodyapi śni.
          Sdodyapi śni.
          Tka waŋna ake ecipaś
         kiya uŋkupi
        ecineś
       hekta ehaŋna
      eyapi taku
     owas ecipaś
    hdi
   ce e.

Going Back

"Back home" implies a return, a cycle of returning, as if it is expected, natural, a fact of life. Families gathered around kitchen tables, connections to generations before us, journeys we make to or away from home. It is there, back home, where we laugh, and cry, about relatives, meals, loss, fulfillment. It is there, back home, where we are trying to return, where we belong, where the landscape is as familiar as our childhood bed and our mother's hands, where our roots are the deepest. It is there, back home, where I meet strangers with my eyes and my father's smile.

Connection to place is powerful, innate. The word for "mother" and for the earth are the same in Dakota: *ina*. Place names around us— Maŋkato, Owotaŋna, Winuna, Shakpe, Mnisota—repeat the story that this land, this land is where our grandmothers' grandmothers played as children. Sixteen different verbs describe returning home, coming home, or bringing something home. That is how important the homeland is in Dakota. No matter how far we go, we journey back home through language and songs, and in stories our grandparents told us to share with our children.

"Back home" for my grandmother is where she was born, where she left in search of work, where she went with her "Indian suitcase," a brown paper grocery bag, to visit her sisters every chance she got. When I was big enough to go with her, each time we passed it, she pointed out the "old home place" marked only by tall pines in the rolling hills along Highway 100. When she retired and moved back home, each time we passed it, I pointed out the "old home place" to my children. The last time we travelled that way together, much to my surprise, my son said, "Look, Mom! There's the old home place!" "Back home" is where my grandmother and my mother are now buried.

When my son returned from his second tour in Iraq, I traveled to the Marine Corps base in Twentynine Palms, California. During his deployment, I sent Sunday comics and wrote of changing seasons and landscape, a small gesture, but a hopeful one to keep him connected to home. Military homecomings are greatly anticipated and highly emotional. Anxious families waiting, waiting, counting the months, then days, then hours and minutes until we see with our own eyes our sons spill out of nondescript white buses in a stream of desert camouflage so wide even a mother can hardly distinguish one Marine from another. When I saw his smiling face emerge through the crowd, then I knew my son was, at last, "back home."

Now, back home is along the Maple River among tall oaks where blackbirds sing. It is where our nearest neighbor brought freshly baked cookies a few days after we moved in. It is where I can stop along the roadside to buy fresh sweet corn and tomatoes and leave payment in a yellow box. It is where the names of towns echo our presence on this land—Blue Earth, Sleepy Eye, Good Thunder. It is a long ways from the "old home place" and the California desert, but there is a kitchen table and a familiar landscape. How do we reconcile that famous quote "You can never go home again" with the end of *The Wizard of Oz* when Dorothy learns she always "had the power to go back" home? Whether it is a place we seek, a sense of belonging, a welcome from those who knew us first, we go back home again and again, traveling, always traveling in search of stories about who we are and where we came from—back home.

Migration

The windows vibrate
as their voices
reverberate
through the trees behind the house
filling the ravine with their chatter
and the clatter of
their wings
warming and drying
in the morning sun
moving the air around
themselves as their calls
grow louder and faster cheering
with anticipation for the arrival of
some yet unseen occurrence and
caught up in the excitement
I rush out and am
stunned
by the volume of their cries
and the trees in full bloom
shimmering black and alive
glimmering with bursts of red
and yellow and in
an instant
as if on
a single command
tens of thousands
of blackbirds
take flight within my reach
pulsating the air around
me as their beating wings
lift my fears away
the sky grows dark

and becomes an ocean
of songs
I have never
heard before.

Wowicak'u

Wowihaŋbde nitawa kiŋ
waci aupi kte
k'a owicayakiya
oyakihi kte.

Heuŋ
waci aniupi
ecineš owicayakiya
oyakihi
eciŋpi.

Okini
niwašteȟ ca
niceca.

Below the Surface

A blackbird calls
as I round the last bend,
familiar melody in
its song.
Ištaoḥdi.

Nothing knocks down
the dust in my throat
kicked up along the road
I used to know well.
Ištaoḥdi.

Fleeting shadows
among trees,
along creeks and bluffs,
carry names filled with
more than history.

In a landscape shaped
by shifting rivers and roads,
stories surface like stone tools
along river banks after
a heavy rain.

Off the highway
marked with red and yellow
on an abandoned map,
I can hear the song.
Ištaoḥdi.

Whispers of mourning doves
echo across

the ravine like evening
prayers.
I am thirsty and
I know the way home.

Daḳota Alphabet and Orthography

This book uses a Daḳota orthography created by and currently used at the University of Minnesota Daḳota Language program. This orthography is one of many used by Daḳota, Naḳota, and Laḳota speakers. All written forms of Daḳota are useful in learning the language.

LETTER	SOUND
a	as in *father*
aŋ	as in *honk*
b	as in *boy*
c	*ch* sound, soft (unaspirated) as *g* in *gel*
ç	*ch* sound, hard (aspirated) as in *chop*
c'	*ch* sound with a pause (glottal stop) before a vowel
d	as in *dog*
e	as *a* in *face*
g	as in *go,* only used when *k* is contracted (e.g., waŋyaka to waŋyag)
ġ	guttural *g* sound, like a growl
h	as in *help*
ḣ	guttural *h* sound, similar to Spanish *x* in *Mexico*
i	as *e* in *me*
iŋ	as in *ink*
k	soft (unaspirated), pronounced like *g* and *k* together
ḳ	hard (aspirated) as in *kite*
k'	*k* sound with a pause (glottal stop) before a vowel
m	as in *mom*
n	as in *noon*
o	as in *go*
p	soft (unaspirated), pronounced like *b* and *p* together
p̣	hard (aspirated) as in *pop*

p'	*p* sound with a pause (glottal stop) before a vowel
s	as in *say*
ṡ	*sh* sound as in *shine*
t	soft (unaspirated), pronounced like *d* and *t* together
ṭ	hard (aspirated) as in *top*
t'	*t* sound with a pause (glottal stop) before a vowel
u	as in *food*
uŋ	as in *tune*
w	as in *water*
y	as in *yell*
z	as in *zebra*
ż	as *z* in *seizure*

to Julie Loehr, Elise Jajuga, and Michigan State University Press for making it all real.

Bernard "Bud" Hirsch was always in my corner as teacher, mentor, and friend, and the first person to call me a poet. His words of encouragement helped me through my years at the University of Kansas and continue to guide me today. Miçaksiça Kicidowaŋ, wicoie dena çic'u.

Glenn Wasicuna has shown me the power of our beautiful language and made me thankful for every day of our life together. Waŋna taku owas wašte.

And for my children, Travis and Erin—may you always know the way home.

Glossary

"Henana Epe Kte"

Henana Epe Kte	*That Is All I Will Say*

"Genetic Code"

Hekta ehaŋna ded uŋțipi.	*Long ago, we lived here.*
Heuŋ he ohiŋni uŋkiksuyapi kte.	*We will always remember that.*
Aŋpetu dena ded uŋțipi.	*Today we live here.*
Heca ohiŋni uŋdowaŋpi kte.	*We will always sing.*

"Journey"

Toked yauŋ he?	*How are you?*
Hekta oko	*Last week*
Uŋspemakiya	*Teach me*
Aŋpetu kiŋ de	*Today*
ake waŋçiyake	*again I see you*
k'a	*and*
çaŋte mawašte.	*I am happy.*

"Delisted"

Ake wambdi kiŋ hdi.	*Again the eagle returns.*
Wambdi kiŋ uŋkicidowaŋpi.	*We sing for the eagle.*

"Root Words"

Maka kiŋ etaŋhaŋ uŋhipi.	*We come from this land.*
Daķota wicoie k'a iapi teuŋĥiŋdapi.	*We treasure our words and language.*
Ikçe wicašta teuŋĥikapi.	*We are mighty.*

"Ḣe Keya Woabdakedaŋ"
    Ḣe keya woabdakedaŋ.   *Turtle Mountain peace.*

"Why He Teaches the Language"
    Wašte do.   *That's good.*

"Morning Song"
    Waŋ! De miye.   *Look! I am here.*
    De uŋkiye.   *You and I are here.*
    Waŋna mitakuye hdipi.   *Now my relatives are coming home.*

"Owotaŋna Sececa"
    Owotaŋna Sececa   *Linear Process (it seems straight)*

"Wowicak'u"
    Wowicak'u   *Feed Them*

"Below the Surface"
    Ištaoḣdi   *[the sound a blackbird makes]*

ACKNOWLEDGMENTS

The journey that this book of poems portrays has been a long and arduous one that could not have been completed on my own.

I am grateful to the editors of the following publications where my poems have previously appeared in print or online in different versions: "Where the Buffalo Roam," "Root Words," and "Awakening" in *Natural Bridge* (Fall 2011); "Dakota Odowaŋ" and "Wowicak'u/Feed Them" in *Water-Stone Review* (2010); "Going Back" in *A View from the Loft* (2009) and in *Mni Sota Makoce: The Land of the Dakota* (Minnesota Historical Society Press, 2012); "Dakota Odowaŋ" and "Ḣe Keya Wo'okiye" in *Yellow Medicine Review* (Spring 2007).

My utmost appreciation goes to The Loft Literary Center in Minnea[...] where I participated in the Native American Inroads prog[...] emerging writers in 1997 with Diane Glancy and again in [...] Susan Power. Ten years later I was honored to be the ment[...] of incredibly talented young American Indian write[...] Native American Inroads program. The Loft has tr[...] sanctuary for me.

The Turtle Mountain Writers Workshop ch[...] and 2007, when Louise Erdrich and Heid E[...] *the Blackbirds* as a book and pushed m[...] words. Chii miigwech!

I am also thankful to James C[...] to get me out of the "emergi[...] patiently waited and waite[...]